THE ONES
WE DIDN'T
KILL

THE ONES WE DIDN'T KILL

A Collection of Poetry and Spoken Word

PJ

PHOENIX JAMES

THE ONES WE DIDN'T KILL

First Edition: 2022

ISBN: 978-1-7396788-2-1 (Paperback)
ISBN: 978-1-7396788-3-8 (Ebook)

Cover Artwork & Design by Phoenix James.
Book Design & Formatting by Phoenix James.

Visit the author's website at www.PhoenixJamesOfficial.com or email him at phoenix@PhoenixJamesOfficial.com

DEDICATION

There's a saying
That you must
As a writer, an artist
As a creative person
Learn to *kill your darlings*
To let go and abandon
Your precious creations
To cast them aside
And not look back
In order to become better
To somewhat clear the way
And make the necessary room
For your really great work

There's a young boy
I've come to know very well
Who a long time ago
I told this idea to

He believed in it for a time
And despite its total truth
Embraced it but not completely
He obviously believed like I do now
That they were worth preserving
And I now, in his honour
Don't feel I have the right not to

And so, hopefully with his blessing
I've come to, I feel, a worthy compromise
To bury them all here, within these pages

They are the ones we didn't kill.

CONTENTS

ALCHEMY FLUID

What can you say to me
The magic man of poetry
Who's the wizard with the flow
There's only one
You know it's me
So you're supposed to be
Proposing a toast to me
Right now
It's me you need to enquire about
Solidified
Is my ninth life on the mic now
But let's get it right now
I never die now
If anything
Like a phoenix I rise now
And fly now
And if you don't believe it
Soon you will find out
Because that's what I'm about
Have you ever seen a nicer rhyme writer
Listen, if I like ya'
I might invite ya'
To my midnight cypher
But don't come with ya' lighter

Because I already burn fire
I done told the devil he's a liar
Got to give it to him though
He's one hell of a trier
But not like me
The poets and MCs are not hot like me
Though they try to be
Cannot write like me
Recite or rock mics like me
But yet they get props like me
But that's all right by me
Witnessing my influence inspires me
I love the way I do it
With an abundance of the fluid
A whizz kid among students
Who need walking through it
Talking through it
This is my blackboard
And I know how to put my chalk into it
So call me, Professor Bored-Of-It
And see me with your rhyme book after
class
So we can sort through it
I mean all of it
Because I'm appalled with it
At this rate

You'll never make the grade
To graduate to the next stage
You're too soft
I was jumping off
Long before
You even knew what a mic was
I don't do private lessons
But we could do some at the right cost

This is alchemy fluid
Let me show you how I do it
Do it with acappellas
Or do it with music
Formulate the flow
So you can't refuse it
And watch it turn to gold
As you take a few sips

I don't even need to flow
I was born poetic
That's why every poet on the globe
Has got to respect this
Every MC
Every lyricist
With a gift to spit
Has got to learn this

Whatever your concern is
I'm still that wordsmith
Worth working with
And I earned this
From years of dedicated service
Stepping against it
Is not worth it
I'll leave the first kid
Immersed in verbal curses
Roaming around
Wondering where earth is
And that's just scratching the surface
I burn verses
Voice box stays hot like a furnace
It's pyromaniac rap
Hot stuff
I heat words and serve them up
More than enough
So pass me your cup
So you can sip, sip a bit
As I flip the script with it
It's British
But not your average fish and chips
In fact it's a far more exquisite dish
Because I'm a lyric specialist
I'm a chef with it

Why mess with it
If you can't manage it
I'm one of the best with it
Why challenge it
I'm a sweet feast
To a rhyme analyst
And what I bring to the table
Will leave your plate up for analysis
You can't fuck with the black alchemist
I'll have you spitting words backwards
You're alien to this
Better phone home
Tell them I spit
On Ukrainian stone carrier ships
And I don't lip sync
I sink lip
And wash my face
In a sacred lake in Egypt
You're not equipped
For my penmanship
And if you don't know
You better ask your Bro
About me 'yo
And tell all your friends
They can see me at the next show

This is alchemy fluid
Let me show you how I do it
Do it with acappellas
Or do it with music
Formulate the flow
So you can't refuse it
And watch it turn to gold
As you take a few sips

Where should I draw the line
Your rhymes are borderline
That's why bored am I
Whenever you start to rhyme
I was born to shine
My rhymes are like fine wine
Flavour for your mind
That only matures over time
Are you sure
You can endure with mine
MC please
I've got a whole lab full of the goodies
And believe
You aren't ready for these
Picasso flows
No, this Matisse
Is not your standard piece

6

Feel me breathe
And caress the canvas like a tease
As I speech paint the picture with ease
From any angle it needs
After surveying the landscape for weeks
Going days without sleep
I'm away
But my name remains in the street
They say I'm deep
They say I'm unique
They say they don't know
It's just the way that I speak
The way that I keep
Surpassing these freaks
With each masterpiece
And when I pass
Please
Don't speak behind my back
No, cease the chat
Please
Don't give me cause to react
Because when I return the attack
You won't like what comes back
Be warned
I'm a brat
I don't only spit on tracks

I shit on tracks
In fact
I stink of hot shit
And what I've concocted is toxic
Got me so sick
One whiff
Will knock you for six
Drop you to your knees quick
I do it too much
You don't do it enough
On nights when you're sexing
I'm up rehearsing my stuff
And I haven't got time
To be stealing ideas, bro
My own are too sweet
And I got so many, boy
I've barely got time to sleep
Time to eat
Barely got time to piss
But when your CD does drop
I'll probably urinate all over the disc
My rhymes are state of the art
Your lines are makeshift

This is alchemy fluid
Let me show you how I do it
Do it with acappellas
Or do it with music
Formulate the flow
So you can't refuse it
And watch it turn to gold
As you take a few sips.

CONSUMABLE LOVE

Loved Big Macs
Loved Chicken Nuggets
Loved Fillets
Loved Fries

Loved Cheeseburgers
Loved McMuffins
Loved Pancakes
Loved Apple Pies

Loved Banana Milkshakes
Loved Caramel Sundaes
Loved Fanta
Loved Coke
With no ice

Loved Snickers
Loved Mars
Loved Maltesers
Loved Chocolate Gateau
Slice after slice

Loved Cheese
And Egg Mayonnaise Bagels

Loved plain Mayonnaise
Within easy reach at the table

Loved Cod
Loved Steak & Kidney Pie
Loved Kebabs
Loved Hot-dogs

Loved Sausage in Batter
Loved lots of Salt on the Chips
Loved Zinger Burgers
Loved Spicy Wings
Loved Spare Ribs

Loved more and more Cakes
Especially craved for Mr Kipling
Long before I changed
And gained more discipline

I found myself hypnotised
And taken into stores
Where I was surrounded
And mind raped
By these denatured hoards
Of processed
Synthetic junk foods

Did I know?
Yes I knew
What damage to the human body
This gunk could do
But was being seduced
By all this mass media coverage
Promotional ads on special offers
And packs of crap they smothered me with
These commonplace authoritarians
These FDA barbarians
It's no wonder all the wise men
And women I know
Are vegans and vegetarians
I loved Chicken Foot Soup
Loved Beef Stew
Loved Roast Lamb
Love fried Flying Fish
And Curry Goat too

But from now on
When I'm coming through

You better stay
Well behind your counter
And maybe even lock up your shop
Or restaurant door

Because I do not love them
Anymore.

CONVERSATIONS OF EMANCIPATION

When I was a child
A Filipino female
Told me to stay away from the crowd
Back then I couldn't break it down
But I understand now
This is the point of my awakening
Amongst the multitudes lost in sin
I seek a righteous thing
And try to take it in
I feel a great weight lift from within
I begin to study the wind
As it blows through the trees
And the rubbish in the streets
My thoughts are deep and discreet
As I watch the birds
Fly high above the church
I look to the clouds
And feel in tune with the earth
Once more I explore the core
And travel the minds pathways
On a pilgrimage to find brighter days
To light the ways
Where the darkness stays
I become amazed

As the distorted becomes visible
I see the reality
And the division of my people
I see the truths that were unequal
Turn weak and feeble
I begin to reminisce
On things far from bliss
I remember this
Yes, I remember this
Once stripped of our wardrobes
And placed in chains
Our forefathers
Were separated under slave names
Our language was changed
And our land was claimed
By evil men with aims
Only to achieve personal gain
Centuries
Of ancestral pain and strain
Runs through my veins
As I walk through these concrete streets
With a solemn face
Trying to find my place
I'm a sole warrior
A solitary soldier
In these times of confined minds

Can't condemn mine
I'm a man of a clan
Of one-hundred and forty-four thousand
The mentally dead are only asleep
I came to arouse them
Arise you, townsmen
And awaken
As if you were one of the chosen
Ready to be taken
Comprehend my conversations
Of emancipation

As the apostles and the prophets
Are gathered
For the coming of the apocalypse
By higher forces
Known and unknown to man
I'm ordained like Abraham
To give positive enlightenment
For your personal development
I bring progressive elements
In rhyme form
Dismiss all irrelevance in a brainstorm
Brandishing a sacred scroll
And a key to life
As my eyes rise to the dark skies

With no surprise
As to what is exemplified
Before me
Bright lights and voices calling me
Doesn't bore me
Let me tell you a story
There's no unity right now
We're all separated in nudity right now
Exposed to the elements of the jinn
I'm staying focused and disciplined
In this sin I'm living in
As I fight this state of sleep
Trying to stay awake
On a quest to reach the holy gate
Before it's too late
Do whatever it takes
Sever and amputate
The negative head of a snake
Not to mention a fake
Witness my acts of faith
As I turn spiritual devils
Into waste
And learn new ways
Because no two days
Are ever the same on this plain
It's insane

It's enough to alter any man's brain
Know your Abel from your Cain
Or be slain
I'm trying to reach the youth before they do
All chaos, confusion and hell will break
loose
But I'm protected
By the armours of my forefathers
Like Ephesians 6
Equipped with lyrical stones and sticks
My mum used to tell me not to spit
But I've got to do it
Got a lot to get off my chest
Won't rest
Until my metaphors alleviate the stress
On men's brains
And eliminates the pain of nations
Comprehend my conversations
Of emancipation

I rise before the break of daylight
Meditate and take a vow like a Nazarite
To keep God in sight
Taking the time to get it right
With a perfectionists plight
The rhyme takes me deep into the night

Into the realms of the unknown
Switch off my phone
Can't afford to be interrupted
While I'm home alone
Constructing a poem that'll blow 'em
I let my mind roam
High performance mode
Every line forms a code
As I take control
Of this instrument of ink that I hold
And stroll
As if effortless across the page
In an attempt to free my people
From the mental cage
Of what seems like an infectious
Materialistic plague
But some begin to rebel and rage
Far too heavily engaged
To accept any change
I wonder can a man be saved
Or is my aim in vain
But then I hear a voice
Calling out my name
I rise again and bare the strain
And endure
Because I've been assured

Here lies the cure
So I write some more and soar
To heights that are hard to reach
Within my speech is the evidence
Of things most benevolent
To your frame of reference
Progressive elements
Are clearly my preference
In a world where the serpent
Seeks to maintain its dominance
In these last days
Fighting to prolong its prominence
Amongst us righteous ones
Who have awakened
And quest to see where we come from
We hear the calling of the distant drum
Our healing has begun
And can't be undone
Our inner most light
Now shines as bright as the sun
And glares in the bare face of evil
People
It's time for us to unite together
Because only together
Can we face this stormy weather
We're in a blizzard that blisters

Brothers and sisters
As we approach
The end time for liberation
Comprehend my conversations
Of emancipation.

COSMIC WORDSMITH

Whenever
I put pen to paper
These lyrics flow
With perfect simplicity
And how I write
With such melodic lucidity
Even to me
Still remains a mystery
But I will be recognised
In history
Eminent
For my impeccable delivery
And ability
You see
My rhymes
Contain astounding intricacy
And amazing vivid imagery
Must be too vivid for some
Because it's as though
Poets don't seem to see
What this is to me
That I've injected
My whole being into this
And that trying to extract me from it

Would indeed in fact be useless
Fruitless
The truth is
The level I maintain
Is hard to attain
And most poets
Don't even come close to
Even the lower parts
Of the heights I aim
So you better be prepared
To work hard
If you ever wish to bear comparison
To yours truly
The highly challenging
Because anytime I step to the stage
And take the microphone
To recite a poem
It's as if the heavens open
I'm well received
I leave poets barely coping
Hoping it won't be noticed
That because of me
Their confidence begins to seize up
Like I lessen their degrees
To the point
That when it's time

For them to step to the mic
And execute some verbal dexterity
They just freeze up
Because within less than three minutes
Of my conversation
I leave poets shaking from the knees up
Realising that it's senseless
To try and fight the intensity
With which I flow
Realising that to reach this height
They've got a long way to go
And that day by day
My level of density just grows and grows
So if you're thinking
You can just
Step to this mic
And just sweep me to the side
Then it means
You need to be demystified
Because anytime I grace this mic
It's a landslide
Caused by rhymes laced with dynamite
That I ignite every time I face this mic
Because you see
In this lives a science
And through its insight and appliance

The universe gives compliance
To my every wish and desire
Causing an alliance with the very fire
Which is my mind body and soul
Time to recognise a power to behold
And pay homage
To prolific lyrics and flows
That accelerate at such a rate
That they would take
Decades
To duplicate and compose
And even then
May not even come close
Close to those who are a host
Of a multitude of modern day Picassos
Who use minds as our canvas
On which we paint poetic pictures
From poetic scriptures
And poetic stanzas
Verses and prose
Let us delineate your thoughts
In alignment with the cosmos
Let us represent you in a light
That shines bright like the sun glows
Let us evoke a drawing of your inner spirit
So vivid

It causes it to erupt like volcanoes
Let us depict the very essence of your soul
And trace it right back
To the precursors of the ancient Pharaohs
See, God knows
This was meant to be
And you can find me
Floating in metaphoric time ships
Designed to make minds flip
Equipped with rhymes to spit
More intricate than Sanskrit
Can you handle it?
Phenzwaan
The cosmic wordsmith.

DECLARATION AFFIRMATION

I'm a shining star
Coming from far
I reach you by quasars
Outshine any new car
Operating by solar
To reveal who you really are
Come up against ours
And face an immeasurable driftage
We came so souls would be lifted
You can't fuck with the gifted
Mic addicted and can't resist it
Names become unlisted when I twist this
I dismiss the swiftest
Aura spreads quick like radiation sickness
Can't forget this once detected
The respected
Microphone mischievous
Turning a lyricist delirious
Deep and deadly serious
Crowd provoker
Far from a joker and no hoper
Put me up on the rota
As professional performing artist
An artist professionally performing

You only need to listen to get drawn in
My voice is like a calling
Or like an abyss you can fall in
It's far from boring
There's just no ignoring
The formula
You've just become absorbed in
Without warning
I wake up in the morning
Yawning
And brainstorming
I'm all in.

DOMINO EFFECT

Some people have got no respect
So I feel no regrets
Rolling up my sleeves
To lay out a domino set
You all follow one another
Like one-two step
Then you fall down
Like what did you expect
Fooling around like clowns
And now you're vexed
But don't be mad at me
If anything I inspire you
Should be glad for me
I'm the reason they hire you
I opened up the scene
So you could sell CDs
Like I do
And that's how you treat me
For guiding you
That's so disrespectful
So disgusting
You're so forgetful
Now you want to discuss things
But we can speak

When you're a little less local
Than Brixton
Try Belgium
Try Budapest
Try Barbados
Try Bermuda
Talk to me about shows
And CD distribution
Then
Talk to me
When your award history
Matches mine
Until such time
You're still borderline
Let's speak again
When you can say you truly shine
At anything
Holla when
It's your ninth time round the bend
Talk to me then
I'm no TV idol
But you don't have to look far
To see what I do
And every week
New poets ask me about the scene
I tell them the truth

I tell them it's all good and nice
If you don't walk around blinded
Thinking poets are the nicest
It's no different from how life is
On the outside some say
A smile is priceless
But on the inside
They're calculated
Cold
Dull and lifeless
Like Murder Mile is
Where I live
Where gunshots
Are not surprises
So much so
That you'd look outside anytime
And still see gun smoke as it rises
And it's no joke
We witness businesses open and close
Like eyelids
And these days
No-one knows
If it's the black or the white kids
Nowadays
We act and look so alike it's
Also why we die

It's too many movies
Too much hard music
Too much hard living
Too many stressed
And too many
Messed up by the system
Too many in prison
Too many drinking
Too many smoking
Too many hooked on drugs
Too many not noticing
Like it's no thing
Too busy posing
No love
Just clubs
Clothes and rims
Fancy phones and diamond rings
And chains
Who needs change in the street
With a pocketful of change in the street
Why make complaints
When you can just change streets
And roll by
Too high to campaign for peace
For another innocent young brother
Slain by police

A mother and family
In pain and grief
Suffering for something
For which there's really no pain relief
Can I speak
They've got posters up right now
All over the underground
Warning us about animals
Becoming endangered species
How they need to be protected
How come there's no posters telling us
How to protect young black boys
From some of these police
From getting shot
Or stabbed
That needs to be corrected
Where's the warning posters for that
Because we're also very endangered
We're also becoming extinct
Maybe we're not as precious as the animals
What's the saying?
Three fifths of a human?

DON'T LET GO OF A GOOD THING

Listen
The party ain't started
Until I'm part of it
Some come close
But don't know the half of it
I'm right up in the heart of it
For those who want the real
And not the counterfeit
I get exited
When it comes to microphones
Because I know
I can recite my funky poems
When it's time
I get right within my zone
With a rhyme
That's more than good to go
Any chance
For me to implement my flow
I'll be there
Like the Jacksons
Act like you know
Because this for me
Is ecstasy at its peak
Have you ever heard

Something so unique
This one
Will have them dancing in the street
It's another one
That just can't be beat
So elementary
But yet so sweet
Little Tanya just can't keep control
Because this vibe is life to her soul
She's dancing but she can't believe
A poet musician
Could feel like me
She says she tries
So hard to express
The joy she feels
So deep in her chest
With every step
But has never yet
You see
With me
You get no less than top quality
Because second best
Is not what I want to be
I rather rock this mic
Than win the lottery
Because high achievement

Sure means a lot to me
That's why when I do this
I do it properly
Because anything less than my best
Is not my policy
Honestly.

ENTRY IS NOW OPEN

Entry is now open
Blessed
Are these words
That are spoken
This is just a token
Of my appreciation
For coming to the club
With the Dark Foundation
To spread a little positive
Vibrational conversation
The nation's realisation
Is our key to elevation
Let these words endureth
Through all generations
Progressive elements
Are at your station
A man
Who thinks he can
Therefore the better man
For a master plan
Check my autonomy
I'm a lot more
Than a wannabe
MC

And if I'm to be
The dignitary
Then so let it be
I take full responsibility
With the gods reigning over me
How could I possibly face defeat
It's only victory
Let me speak
I'm into big things
That some consider deep
On a serious quest
To reach the mountain peak
The road that I travel
Is both rocky and steep
But just like the stronger ones
I stay on my feet
Trying to reach
The minds of the weak
Find the lost sheep
My soul to keep
Indeed
It's like a job that I can't leave
Let's proceed.

FOOLISH MORTALS

Indeed
It was me
Who tied up the first missing poet
And hung him by his feet from the tree
After stripping him naked
Took a pair of pliers
And wrenched out six of his teeth
Sliced holes in his flesh
And cut his tongue out
With the broken pieces from his own CD
After that
Yes, I did leave
But then came back with a rusty axe
Chopped his head off and watched it bleed
Put it in a box
And sent it to his family gift wrapped
For Christmas eve
Reporters always leave out the crucial facts
When they tell my stories
And I hate that
Please
The second poet never made it to the
hospital
He was dead

Long before the call was received
Besides
Even if he was alive at the time
He couldn't speak
I tied him up in his basement
And force fed him
With the pages from his poetry book
And made him eat
Until his stomach burst
He couldn't breathe
I told him
It could be worse
If they have poetry readings in hell
At least now you'll remember the words
The third
Must've sensed his death coming
He started running
When I summonsed him to my dungeon
Requesting that he and his friends come in
So I could show them something
Their attempts to escape were in vain
All but for one thing
I chopped them up in my bathtub
Letting their blood escape down the drain
After dumping their clothes
I liquidised their remains

Added milk and other ingredients
And made a shake
Another of their friends came knocking
I said
Take a seat
They're on their way
You'll see them soon
Have a drink while you wait
It's homemade
He said
Thanks
It tastes great
How long did it take to make
I said
Not long
Your friends helped me make it
And you
You're going to help me make a cake
With his remains
I also made bread and biscuits
Then invited more writers around
And fed them with it the next day
And there were five not four
I wish these journalists
Would get my story straight
Anyway

I didn't like what they had to say
So I killed them in the same way
And gave what I made
To the audience at a showcase
I organised back in May
The next one that went missing
Was also a poet
She was the third female
Caught her whispering
At a poetry reading
Instead of listening
She was speaking
At the back
I didn't like that
When she got up to go the toilet
I followed her in
And strangled her with her head wrap
Locked the cubicle from the inside
Climbed out
Waited
Until everyone left the venue after the show
And I came back
Disposed of her body
In an old storage cupboard outside the
toilet
She obviously had a lot to speak about

So I left her with her mobile phone
Sealed the door and went home
I didn't want to spoil it
Oh
And the newspapers didn't say so
But it was me who killed the promoter
Who they found disfigured
Floating in the river
He promised once again
He'd pay me that night
But he didn't
So after the show
I kidnapped him
Tied his hands up and set him alight
At first, he thought I was kidding
But the look in my eyes made him realise
No he isn't
I'm going die
Especially when I came back
To the house from outside
With a petrol can
And dragged him into the kitchen
Afterwards
His burnt body was still twitching
I rolled him into a rug
And lifted him onto my shoulder

I then drove his body
To the end of the bridge
And threw him over
These news people
Really need to get sober
And print the right stuff
And stop making such a mess
Of my write-ups
Are they drunk?
I didn't kill the host in a mad rage
I was calm when I did it
I choked him
With a microphone cord backstage
Plus I spoke to him first
I was very sane
I calmly explained
That this is what happens
When anyone mispronounces my name
That was his end
I finally covered his body over
With the curtain
And went back into the crowd again.

GET HIGH

With each new verse
I become more of an addict
And my only concern
Is how I can feed my habit
And all you need to learn
Is that there are those
Who have to have it
Starving artists
But that's not too tragic
The tragedy is
Those who aren't hungry enough
To grab it
Have no vision
Forward thinking or foresight
Can't manage
No drive
They die inside
Disparaged
Realising this life
Promises no horse and carriage
No palace
You can sit this one out on the side
Drying your eyes
I'll be outside

Waiting on the chariots
With my sword and my chalice
Filled with Irish Mist
And a Coconut Kiss
I can handle this
What if I die
No
I speak no such languages
I only learnt two things
Can't only really exists in the mind
And never say die
I will survive
When the smoke clears
They'll see me
Hat to the side
Riding out from the ruptured saloon
After things go boom
High as a kite
Whistling
Singing
Don't mess with my money or my mic
Saddle bags packed with riches
Strapped to the side
Of a horse named spirit
Giddy-up, giddy-up
What do these cowards

Know about sacrifice
All they know about is giving up
I've been getting high for ten years
And I still ain't high enough
How long can you strive
Just to get by enough
On the streets selling your stuff
Like drugs
It's deep
Supplying the cut
Creating a buzz
And watching the demand go up
Trying to keep your feet on the ground
But getting high
Because you didn't realise
They would feel it so much
And that you'd be dealing so much
Now you're hiring guys
To package and wrap it
Yes
Me and my hustle go together
Like carrots and rabbits
But it's no hat-trick
More like voodoo magic
No top hat and cloak
No cards

No gadgets
I speak spells
If you listen well
You'll catch it
Every time my CD sells
I inebriate myself
As well as someone else
Getting high off the vibe
These spirits provide
I'm just the vessel
Only the lyrics are mine
I'm just the witness
I listen to the guides
Couldn't quit if I tried
Tried and almost died
Some gifts come with a price
If staying addicted
Is keeping away the sickness
I'd rather stay high
Lifted
Intoxicated out of my mind
Because that's the only time
I'll know
I'm alive.

GONNA BE SOMEBODY

You only get one chance
So try not to waste it
Here comes mine
And I think I'll take it
And no matter what they say
Or do to try to hold me back
My train is success bound
And it won't fall off the track
Now, I'm a shining star
And before I start
I'd like to say a few words
In your behalf
You see I believe
We can have anything we want in life
As long as we are able to rise
Above the strife
And those that are seeking
The surrender of our dreams
Inside us
We already have the means
In fact we've got all we need
Focus and discipline
Those are the keys
That'll keep us free from negativity

That's why I read
And roll to studios
And put down flows
Like nobody knows
Like there's no tomorrow
Or nowhere else left to go
Wearing the same clothes
I wore the day before
Because nothing even matters no more
But the cause I'm flowing for
I just want to make more tracks
I just want to write you more raps
So I can get more feedback
I want everybody saying I feel that
I hope they feel this
It's just something with a little twist
Just a little positive lyrical injection
To spice the track up
So for every time they turn it down
You'll just turn it back up
Because it's positive stuff
And just what you need
When you're feeling
Like you've had enough
Like the old man
That just sits down by the corner

And watches the world go by
I often wonder why
He's even lost the desire to try
But who knows
Maybe one day he'll hear my words
And change his mind
Meanwhile
I'll just keep smiling
And climbing up the ladder
Until I reach the top
Even though the things I've got
Are not a lot
I still endure
And further more
Let this be like my wall of gratitude
Saying thank you to all of you
For putting in
All the positive input
That you have done and that you do
Thank you
From the bottom of my heart
I know you'll be there until the end
Because you were there from the start.

INCOGNITO AND DEBONAIR

Incognito
And perfectly debonair
I soar into the air
I'm the masked sky rider
Dweller above the high-risers
High flyer in the art of disguises
It's a bird
It's a plane
No
It's the heart of surprises
I come in all shapes and sizes
Until I get my poetic licence
And now
With my phonetic science
I'm swooping down
Down
Down
Into the underground
With a sound
Full of verbs and pronouns
So profound
I must be homeward bound
Not lost
So I won't be found

And my descent is not a decline
For now I'm heard
With words and rhyme
And I can climb
Climb
Climb
Through the city streets
Where good and evil competes
Angels and demons meet
Who will be the victor
Who will see defeat
One advantage
I can see them
But they can't see me
For I am like an invisible man
With an invincible plan
To overthrow
And enter in by deception
If there is no reception
Or acceptance as I am
And I can
And will slide past the man
Who stands on the hill
With the time glass
Hide or be killed
By his wrath

I camouflage
And take a new path
They all make me laugh as I pass
They move smooth
But I move too fast
Good thing I've got wings
And a mask.

IT'S COMING

Lyrically coming of age
On each page
And on each and every stage
Came to free the minds of slaves
And get paid
And can only go halfway
On a minimum wage
That's why these books are written
That's why these CDs
Video
And T-shirts were made
So the name is engraved
And will live on
Long after the end of days
Until the end of time
After the kingdom or prison
Of yours and mine
So may your great
Great
Great
Great grand children
Never neglect to tell their next of kin
It's been coming in the trees
It's been coming in the seas

It's been coming in the winds
If you're looking you will see
And you will hear if you're listening
Because it's within
Always has been
Before the birth of our curse
Before the earth
Before the beginning
Now its whispering
It's coming
It's returning
It's rekindling
It's burning
Coming hot
Its coming fast
And it can't be stopped
Its coming untouchable
Coming bold
Sparkling
Shiny and bright
Coming colorful
Red
Yellow
Blue
Purple
And white

56

Coming sexy and explicit
Overly seducing you
To get with it
And before you know it
You've given in
Because it'll reach you
No matter what world you're living in
Something to make your soul dance
Because it's coming
With sacred rhythms in
Even coming pretty pink
With ribbons in
But it's coming
It's coming
In the spirit of ancient melanin
It's coming for everyone
And everything
It's coming in little Phenz
Because I've been telling him
Telling him it's coming
In the form of
Subliminal ink darts
That make you think hard
As they sing
And sting
And stick to your heart

Infinite and eternal
Burning
Coming forever to keep
It's coming deep
And it's coming dark
And its coming black
Because its coming back
Coming back
From always present
Because some things
Are only for a moment
Others
Are eternal
Irremovable in their survival
And that this
Shall endure
Remain
And exist forever
Is undeniable.

LET'S BREAK THE CHAINS

I came
To break the mental chain
Of those absorbed
In the pursuit of material gain
With positive vibrational conversations
The nations realisation
Is our only key to elevation
We're living in an age of information
My brothers and sisters
Study hard
Work smart
And don't be fools
What you don't know
Will hurt you
That's the rule
To be oblivious is uncool
I'm taking us all back to school
With rhymes and melodies
That open minds
And create remedies
If they sometimes
Leave you hypnotised
And dreamy eyed
Let it be of no surprise

I came to save lives
With words from the wise
For it is through lack of knowledge
That my people shall perish
Let wisdom be the thing you cherish
And even though
It seems impossible and hard
To keep a pure mind
And a true heart
Remember
Every successful ending
Begins with a single start
And good timber
Doesn't grow with ease
The stronger the wind
The stronger the trees
My seeds
Please increase
If you don't fight
For who you want to be
Then tell me
Who else are you going to be
There's no limit
To what we can achieve
And find
If we unite minds

Of the same kind
In this race against time
It's imperative we be cautious
But demonstrative
In these last days we live
Creating a greater sense of urgency
In this time of emergency
Emerge with me
Those who know and understand
The final hour is at hand
As we're faced
With the fraudulent ways
Of woman and man
Who prefer to keep
Your true purpose unknown
So the only thing we know
Is phat rides
And mobile phones
And weed spots
The best place to find rocks
When will it stop
My people are starved
In regards to consciousness
With very little food for thought
Taught that only money talks
They visit prison cells and courts

For chasing after
The beauties of the beast
With no relief they decrease
And become without decency
Or decorum
The chosen few
Deliver brief previews for them
In this millennium
Where they'll be less peace
Than rebellion
And no apology
For those
Who forsake this terminology
Or dismiss cross-references
From messengers
Who aim to perpetuate
A positive mind state
Within the youth
And redirect
The unaware and the uncouth
For sinful things are in our region
But all mention remains unintriguing
To the unbelieving
Souls who watch Steven
Speilberg
And don't believe a word they heard

Or a single thing seen on the screen
Such as these sleep deep
But the Prince is always keen
To awaken them from their dreams
With words blessed and sanctified
The truth you cannot hide
It's incontrovertible
It's vertical
Malice may attack it
And ignorance may deride it
But in the end
There it is again my friend
You can't deny it
Or subside it
Although
Some have tried it
Only to find
It can't be undermined
It's too sublime
Like once upon a time
When we used to live peaceful
And righteous
Now we're fighters
And deceitful liars
Womanisers
And drug dealers

Peelers
Prostitutes and players
Drinkers
Non thinkers
Gunslingers
And slayers
We used to spread love
Now we spread hatred
We messed up
We used to be blessed
Now we possess bad luck
We're perverted and corrupt
Stealing from each other
Man and woman
Turn upon their lovers
While unconcerned fathers
Escalate the rate of single mothers
And mediocre brothers
Who fool around
And fall in love
With modern day Delilahs
Are in store for a lot more
Than they desire
We all better wake up
And see past the make up
Or feel the fire.

LYRICAL MURDERER

I am a lyrical murderer on the loose
Ready to die
And ready to tongue tie
Any ten tongues in a noose
Who have misconceived
And led themselves to believe
They are more lethal than me
Oh how foolish they be
Can't they see?
This sickle shaped
Razor blade sharp tongue
When released
Will verbally cut their words up
Piece by piece
And severely sever their egos
Until these beliefs are deceased
As we go
Deep
Too deep
For these shambolic
Shallow souls to keep
Can't hold up
Their roots are too weak
My fruits are too sweet

On branches too far to reach
But still they proceed to compete
Being too proud
They refuse to bow with the meek
As if they don't understand
The powers that be
You could step outside right now
And witness the impact of my raps
Flowing out into the streets
In fact
You could stay right where you are
And be moved off your feet
And off your seats
Because the very sound
And rhythm of my voice alone
Is the drumbeat
And you all act like you don't know it
But that's the reason
Why half these MC's and poets
And lyricists
And wordsmiths
Can't sleep
In fear that they may blow it
And face defeat
After thinking
They were the biggest fish in the sea

Thought they had it locked
But now someone's turning the key
And turning up the heat
I repeat
Turning up the heat
All will suffer severe lyrical burns
Who do not retreat
There's a killer on the rhyme page
So come bring your best speech
And watch me tear it apart
Like hungry lions and fresh meat
Leaving you dead beat
And washed up
Like you were shipwrecked at sea
Because I'm a lyrical murderer
On a verbal killing spree
And once entangled
In my web of words
There's no getting free
Ain't you heard?
It's worse if you struggle
Just let your destiny be
Can't test this deity
As I proceed to devour thee
They say you're guilty of plagiarism
How do you plea?

Now answer carefully
As there will be
No calling of truce
And be reminded
Every line you fly gives me a boost
And that that's why
I'm a lyrical murderer on the loose
Ready to die
And ready to tongue tie
Any ten tongues in a noose
Who have misconceived
And led themselves to believe
That they are more lethal
Than me
Oh how foolish they be.

MESSAGE TO THE HOST

It's at that stage
Where I begin to fully accept
The belief that you won't change
Can't change
That you don't seem to know
Any other way
What you did that day
Was pathetic
Once again
It seems you just don't get it
I've been advised
To just brush it off my shoulder
And forget it
But the more I ignore it
It seems the worse you get
So I need to address it
First of all
Your announcements
Are mispronounced
And I'm not impressed with it
To say the least
You're supposed to be a host
I appreciate that you are a comedian
But when you are dealing with an artist

Whose artform is feeding him
It's not a joke
Your job here
Is to be clear
Concise
And precise
Whilst maintaining
An entertaining night
Thinking less about yourself
And more about how this show might go
If I don't get this next artists name right
Especially if he or she
Is a sensitive performer like me
I often wonder where your focus is
And the real joke is
You probably don't even remember
Holding her three line bio in your hand
Which you couldn't even be bothered to
read
So you gave her some bullshit introduction
As she made her way to the stage
Which completely lowered her self esteem
Fucked up the whole show
For not only her
But also for a room full of good people
Who just paid a decent entrance fee

Who now have to witness her suffer
Because of you
She's on the stage
And all of a sudden
She can't play properly
And she's forgetting words to a song
She's sung every other day
Since her brother died in that plane
And I know exactly how she feels
Because you've done the same to me
On numerous occasions
And it's a shame
Being master of ceremonies
Doesn't say anything
About telling inappropriate jokes
Or playing silly games
And she might not have the courage
To tell you
Might not think it's her place
But I'll be the first
To tell you to your face
How much it's a disgrace
Especially when
My livelihood depends on it
It's time to let you know
Half baked introductions

And mispronounced names
Is simply not good enough
It's shabby
You need to see the importance
And take this more seriously, daddy
And since you got mouths to feed
And bills to pay
Then really you should understand this
Automatically
If not
Takes notes
Or hit the road
Because the next time
You fuck up the details
When you're mentioning an artist
Or their CD
He or she
May not be happy
Especially when your delivery
Sounds so half hearted
We're not feeling it
You need to have more regard
For the artists you're dealing with
Because the next one you diss
Might be harder to reason with
You're a seasoned comedian

Nuff respect
But why request
Info from a performer
If when you get on stage
To introduce them
You're not reading it
That's something you need to check
There's no excuse
And what's worse
Is the times you do read it
But make such a mess
That it leaves me and others
Wondering why you bothered
What's the use
Apart from making my blood boil
It only leaves me to question
Where your level of professionalism
Starts and ends
Especially when
I can contact you
On two separate occasions
And book you to do your comedy set
At two separate events
Both of which you confirmed with me
But both of which you didn't attend
No telephone call

No email
No explanation
For either of them
And even though
You did it on the first occasion
It can happen once
But you don't let it happen again
Twice?
Guess I must be pretty way down
On your importance list
And that's cool
But I assumed at least
You would have been man enough
To do what's right regarding this
Simply because
That's respect
Something we often talk about
When we come to these places
To these stages
Respect for self
Respect for audience
And respect for other artists
So I've been thinking on it
Wondering which part I missed
I didn't come up with any answers
But what I came up with

Was this
And it was inspired by you
So I hope you heed it
Because next time
You're on your way to the venue
To host the show, bro
You might need it.

MIND STATE

Its unlimited power
Became stronger
With every approaching minute
Towards the final hour
Weak brave hearts
Became cowards
Couldn't sustain a place in the race
Against a force as great
As a meteor shower
When it hit
They got devoured
And many came after
Tried to come harder
And faster
But couldn't cause
As much disaster
By the way
Where's the pastor
There's been a change of plan
Send a message to Mary
But don't tell her where I am
Because she won't understand
That I'm a shining star
Coming from far

The mind state
That rides the tracks
Takes you beyond
The universe and back
With a rap
Now comprehend that
It's the same mind state
That creates
And formulates the syntax
In fact
What you can do
Is picture a high level of fortitude
Consider this
For a moment or two
And what it shows
Is the hero of all heroes
The one thing that controls
Each and every man
No matter where he goes
The elevator of souls
The foreteller of the foretold
The soul controlled
Designer of your fate
Puts you up alongside
A long line of greats
Or causes you to stagnate

There's no limits
To what it can destroy or create
It is its own place
And within itself
Can develop hell of heaven
Or heaven of hell
A large mass of nerve cells
With the ability
To collect and connect
More people than Cellnet
Or Vodafone
The same faculty
That made E.T. phone home
Creates its own twilight zones
And makes the vocalist sing
In a high pitch tone
Is it known?
The mind, baby
The mind
My mind
Your mind
Our mind
By special design.

MISSION ANTAGONISED

I walk like an Egyptian
Talk like an Egyptian
Give me the microphone
And I spit preconceived definitions
Into a new position
A rap musician
A poetician
A true man on a true mission
But they don't wish
To see me glisten
Delivering documentation
So vital
That only a fool wouldn't listen
Words so powerful
And essential to your system
That only a fool wouldn't listen
Words so powerful
And essential to your system
That I don't want anyone to miss them
I'm trying to free the minds
From the mental prison
Because it's a global war
Between the princes of peace
And the princes of darkness

We the people didn't start this
It started in the minds of the heartless
Who are soon to be consumed
By their own envy and greed
Thinking they're the smartest indeed
But the law of karma
Pays back in full
You better believe
That's why I sow seeds
And grow trees
Of positivity
The truth hurts
That's why they don't like me
I tell it how it is
And not just slightly
Negativity wants to fight me
But I break it down to its knees
Begging please
I give you just what you need
I've got the keys
And progressive elements
At three-hundred and sixty degrees
You need these
To elevate yourself out
From any disease
Whether it be mental

Physical
Or spiritual
Exalted is he
That receives this lyrical material
And digests it like cereal
And that's the reason why
The devils keep coming
Trying to score points against me
But they can't get one in
I stand supreme
Keep my mind clean
Ain't no make believers
Running on my team
Only real individuals
With real dreams
Who see things
The way they're supposed to be seen
And you should really be glad
I get noticed
But because of your focus
You rather see me hopeless
Like a penny with a hole in it
Lost and broken with no spirit
But there's no limit
To what I can achieve
To me

You're just like the weeds
That lie at the bottom of the sea
Trying to hold me down
So I can't breathe
So I never get to reach the surface
But your attempts
To stifle me are worthless
Didn't know I had a purpose
Only realised it when you heard this
Now you're wordless
Ain't got a thing to say
Only want to stop my productivity
All day
Everyday
But that's okay
Because I'm still going to get paid
Still going to reap the rewards
Still going to be in accord with the lord
Still living reassured
I'm still one of the one-hundred
And forty-four
Still a rebel with a cause
Trying to open closed doors
And reach lost souls
At the cross-roads
It's already been told

There'd be persecution
So just like the sun
I rise above the confusion
And still shine
My solution
Is to keep on moving
If your plight
Is anything like mine
I've seen the hard times
And I'm sure a lot more before it's over
That's why I write these rhymes
To keep a strong mind
And stay sober
In this madness
Seems like sadness
When you're on top
And gladness when you're not
They don't want to see me
Rock the spot
But the fact is
I'm too hot to be stopped
I'm elevating
Concentrating
On making a break
And not waiting
Because people these days

Are too damn fake
And aggravating.

NEVER SAY DIE

I'm at the lab
Preparing to leave
Pen and pad
Microphone in my back pocket
And a bag full of CDs
Navy blue baggy jeans
And a white pair of Nike Air
A hand full of Phenzology flyers
And a maroon Phenzology T-shirt
Website inscribed on the reverse
I'm off to work
Arriving at the place
And gliding onto the stage
I'm like
Just think
Countless shackled slaves
Thrown overboard
Into the ocean to die
It's no surprise
Every time they turn in their graves
They raise the tides
Waves so high
They could wash away land and life
In a day and a night

Oh wind and sea
Why oh why do you cry
Oh why so angry at mankind
What has thou witnessed with thine eye
Whom upon this land doth thou despise
See, the sea never sleeps
Neither the wind nor the skies
Neither the spirits of the tormented
Chained to the seabed
Salt water burning their eyes
Sorry
We tried
And when you're close enough
To lend your attention to the ocean
For long enough
It all makes sense
And is as real
As the existence of life
Spirit never dies
So tell Marcus
His thing
About coming in the whirlwind
Was right
And tell Martin
That the dream is still alive
Tell Marvin

What's going on
And that troubled men still survive
And though we come up hard
Still we rise
Eyes on the prize
Do or die
And whatever he say or she say is cliché
We say
Whatever we like
So take notes
And in these days
We'll say a cliché
A thousand times if it applies
So don't waste time
Trying to analyse that
Which doesn't need to be analysed
You know
Just go with the flow
Jokes aside though
I came to give you something
For your soul
I survive
Just so you might know
That there are survivors
Just so you might leave this place
Inspired

My goal
Is to make you feel what I feel
When I feel the fire
Burning deep in my chest
Like right here
Right now
So much I can barely express my desire
So little time
So many ways
I could say all the so many things
I wish to say
Said so much already
And I feel like
I haven't even opened my mouth to speak
Yet I can feel the electricity
Transferring from my being to yours
Transforming all the negative energy
Within and around us
Don't doubt what you're feeling
Just be sure and glad that it found us
There's absolutely right now
No better place to be
Than paying attention to the voice saying
That whatever the mind can see
The mind can achieve
And that when this is over

And you leave
You will be nothing more or less
Than the sum total of all you believe
So go build a high and fine fortress
Beautiful and bold
Fill it with treasures
Beyond this world
Worth more than diamonds and pearls
More than rubies and gold
Stand guard at the door of your mind
And watch the magic unfold
So much to find
So much untold
So much to explore
Before you touchdown in the end zone
The wonder is in the journey
In the thrill of the unknown
It's in the winning
But more so in the shaping of character
In the time that we're alone
It's in the distance travelled to get there
More than the coming home
So walk with me
No please
Walk with me
One

Two
Three
Step
One
Two
Mic check
Hey
You don't even know the half yet
No wait
Don't even laugh yet
I used to get upset
They used to turn my mic off
Back in the day
Didn't like it when I spoke this way
Which was odd to me
Until I heard the word
That they didn't like poetry
That was spiritual or godly
So it soon became a place not for me
Not because I had plans to leave
But because they tried to close me out
From all prospects and possibilities
Plus they didn't like the fact
That when I came
I already had my own CDs
Which I sold

At my own shows each week
Guess they couldn't hold me
Or mould me
So they confiscated the mic
And set me free
Which had a knock on effect
Clear to see
Because other mics got switched off
And other affiliated cliques
Also suddenly weren't keen
It seems
Artists with dependency issues
Are much closer
To a promoters dream
Indeed
Everybody wants to get on
But cant we all just get along
I mean
Picture the scenario
You've been booked to do a show
About three weeks ago
It's three days before the event
And you've been awaiting
Final confirmation and details
So you decide
To contact the booking agent

To see if you may have missed her call
Or any emails
But she says
No, because after we spoke
When I arrived back at my desk
I said oh
Because I had a message from you
saying you'd cancelled
And couldn't make the show
I said
Yeah?
She said
Yeah!
You sound surprised
So it wasn't you?
I said
No!
Anyway
We sorted it out
And as planned I did the show
That was three years ago
But it's happened a few times since
Moral of the story is
Somebody tried to sabotage my gig
So if your thinking is
That the poetry scene

Is all love and kisses
Then you need to change your thinking
Quick
It's the same notion
As anywhere
Where human beings share emotions
And that's everywhere on the planet
If you're planning on sticking around
Your skin better be thick
And tough like granite
Whatever your profession or intention
Damn it
If you're planning to excel
Then your backbone
Better be able to withstand it
Better have ocean drive
Determination and perseverance
Past a wish list and a bag of chips
Yup, this is it
This is the life you chose
No look higher
This is the life that chose you
Do what you're supposed to do
Fly up high where the eagles fly
Let the mountains hold their peace
Bow not even to the sky

Go beyond your means
See with your eye
What first the mind has seen
Do what others dare not to
Breathe everlasting life into your dreams
And know that the only thing
That matters right now in this scene
Is you
And me
What we're open to receive
And what we're willing to sacrifice
To be free
I am by your side
Rest easy
No Mic Jacker
Can ever Terence Trent me
Believe me
It's not even a factor
Too much strength in my character
That's why I can't keep friends
Who would make better actors
Perhaps it's because they lack substance
And feel they need to pretend
To hide what's missing
But they all get found out in the end
Listen

94

I gave you truths
They tried to twist them
Did all they could do
To try and jeopardise the mission
But like myself
You're wise to their traditions
You see through their disguises
Your knowledge is above their wisdom
You see further than their limited vision
Far enough
To find it in your heart to forgive them
And here we are
Serving one another like it's a religion
I rode by camel
Across the Sahara desert
In search of your treasure
Sailed across the river Nile
Just so I could deliver something
Worth your while
Scaled the pyramids
Just so I could give you this
From the ancient cities I rode through
As a Nubian Prince
Because once you were dubious
But now you're convinced
This is my gift

I'm ecstatic at the fact
That our faith has not wavered
I'm humbled at the thought
That you have been awaiting
My offering with patience
I pray I'll always remain
The subject of your invocation
In how many ways can I say
I am grateful for the invitation
And today as always
I took the scenic route to work
Just so we could enjoy more of this
Precious time together
They say nothing is forever
But look at us
We're eternal
Just as long as we have now
Just as long as we have each other
Just as long as we have this
So many things yet to discover
Let's never forget our wings
Let's always remember how to fly
Without retreat
And without surrender
Let's never
Say die.

NINTH LIFE

With the release of The A.R.T.I.S.T
Is where it all started
The abilities to inspire sacred things
Now I contemplate many CDs later
I'm still easily the favourite target for haters
And spectators
Question who one of the greatest is
When the answer is in their faces
Every time they play my discs
Or whenever I grace these stages
It's as clear as day is
Some say it's
Something like a phenomenon
How he keeps on going on and on
But the truth is
I've been doing this for ages
These are the rhymes I played with
When other minds
We're concentrating
On Nintendo's
And Sega's latest
Games consoles are great
Yes
But all the graphics

And special effects in the world
Couldn't create this
Nope
Not to be played with
It's too sacred
And if you're a fake kid
It'll leave you naked
Exposed
To show what your true nature is
A wise man wouldn't challenge me
Who wants to interfere
With the basis for immortality
And the increase of my talent
Only leaves more casualties
Ninth life
Speaks fluid alchemy
Listen and witness
My right to defeat
Each opposing principality
Existing
For only as long as say they can be
Hope they all got a plan-B
Because I've only just been warming up
Yet it seems they can't handle me
One of the best rhyme writers
This side of the globe

So put that in your magazine
And please tell them who said so
Because these has-beens
Need to know
It takes more than a few poems, yo
To get within a stone throw
Of this philosophers stone flow
And I'll write
Whatever the hell I like
It's my ninth life on the mic
And I've solidified the right
How many times must I tell you
I'm a bird of a different feather
I'm like a phoenix
Writing words
That last forever
Yes
Forever
For ever, ever
Bless these half hearted poets
They try but could never
Surpass me
Need to be a little more clever
A little faster
I take pleasure
In being that poet bro

Running reckless poets off the road
For trying to play me like Connect 4
That's why we don't connect anymore
Ah you thought I'd forget
No, let's explore
What on earth are you really vexed for
Can't be me
I'm out of this world
That's for sure
Ah maybe it's because
People like this poet more
Or maybe it's because you heard
I had a few CDs
Then found out
I actually had a few more
Now you hate me, that's fine
The fact is
You can't subtract from my grind
Detract from my shine
Retract back to your map
Work hard
And you may catch up in time
But oh
I'm too far down the line
Too defined
Boy

You must be outside your mind
Trying to deny my rhymes
What were you thinking
Come on
You must have been drinking
Look
What you need to do
Is log back onto my website
Send a message
And apologise
And tell everyone
It's my ninth life
That it won't happen again
And you didn't mean any harm
Then we'll be straight
There's really no need to hate
It seems we sometimes
Dislike what we can't be like
I feel for you, bro
But I really haven't got time
For the strife
Ninth life
Sending a shout out to all sides
The eastside
Nothing but peace signs
To the westside

Couldn't care less
Who's the best side
Nothing but love for each side
Including the north and south side
No need for us all to divide
Some poets and promoters
Just need to keep their mouths tied
And we can keep it nice, right?
Because I too prefer the sweet side
But it seems some poets and promoters
Prefer the beef side
All because their analysis of me
Reveals no weak side
Enter the ninth life
Witness the rise
And what I speak
Solidified.

NO FEAR

Zero fear when I come
The rising son fears none
I'm Phenzwaan
I'm one of the last ones
My tongue
Resembles a silver sword
Cuts through a fraud
And for all those in discord
With the lord
I raise more hell than Hellraiser
Behold
I'm a lyrical saviour
MC's get writers block
Every time they put pen to paper
I just speak my mind
With rhymes that flow like vapour
Causing convulsions
Of the earth's surface inside your brain
Using a form of mental eugenics
To create change
And awaken the mentally dead
The young and the dumb
Are spoon fed
By these words that are said

This is my pledge
As I stay ahead
Of time
For the mind
Is its own place
And within itself
Can create
Hell of heaven
Or heaven of hell
Because home
Is wherever the mind dwells
Unleashed finally
It's the epitome
Of what I represent
In a time
Where redemption for the mind
Seems far from heaven sent
I'm writing up lyrics
Fed up of gimmicks
And brothers in it to win it
Thinking their all up in it
The right way
But they're not
They don't even come close to
MC's who master ceremonies
Like we're supposed to

Always remembering
What we go through
To get this
I protect this
And never forget
Or respect this
Conditioning via the system
Look at the way we're living
Learning how to take
And losing all knowledge of giving
To each other
Man don't respect his brother
Daily
I'm facing
Mental and physical battles
With negative
But I can't let it live
My mind is too eventful
For any negative
To penetrate its central
It's essential
To control the mental
For behold
The tongue can penetrate a man's skin
From within
Make him think different things

Commit certain sins
Left with no knowledge
Of the time he's living in
The worst sin
You could ever commit
Is to let evil men
Enter inside your mind
And play with it
Stand guard
At the door of your mind
All the time
Watch for signs
And a Phenzwaan
With a silver chain
With a key that shines.

NO FUN HOUSE

First you approach me
To host your weekly poetry show
I figured good for me
Good for poetry
So
We agreed my fee
And were good to go
I would book the feature artists
And we would both promote
You cut my money
I said okay
It's the first night
And things still need to grow
The second time
The words I really wanted to say
Stuck in my throat
The third time
Is third strike
I was ready to blow
Then I thought about
All the artists
I had booked to perform
At the future shows
Wanted to be there

To support them
After they'd flown
So far across the globe
Lugging their cases
Full of CDs
Books
DVDs
And clothes
Coming to greet the masses
And spit their flows
But when we all got to the event
The door was closed
Yes
Guess who left us all
Out in the cold
With no prior warning
And my phone was on
So you definitely weren't calling
So disrespectful
So inconsiderate
So unprofessional
So appalling
And there's me
Receiving complaints
The next morning
And weeks after that too

It's a good thing
There's other shows
These acts could do
Without notice
And the joke is
I've recorded these facts
And still haven't heard back from you
Is that what you do?
They say you're all about yourself
Young
Unprofessional
Guess I didn't know
I was the one defending you
And it seems
That's how it goes
The one who shows
The dog the most love
Is often the one
Who gets bitten on the nose
What did you suppose?
That I didn't have any teeth of my own
No, I don't want to eat
Don't need shoes for my feet
I haven't got no mouths to feed
Haven't got no house to keep
So I'll be a mouse

And let you shit on me
Let you dirty up my name
And have nothing to say
You should know me better
I really don't play.

ORDER FOR THE DAY

I'm like a live wire
A wild fire
That can't be tamed
My mind operates off a source
That goes deeper than my brain
A force you can't contain
For it's far too incredible
Makes the hulk look weak
Minuscule and forgettable
My style is edible
And highly digestible
Like a vegetable
My words penetrate
As I illustrate
And place you in a thoughtful state
Concentrate
As I guide you back
To an essence richer
I paint a fluorescent picture
With language and literature
I take charge of intellectual faculties
With intelligence of a high degree
And a vocal focus
On disciplinary philosophy

I make a man turn off his TV
And listen closely
As I bring forth bread for the soul
Worth more than gold
Behold
Before you
I deliver a bowl
Of sustenance
Containing more substance
Than any recommended
Daily allowance
Eat from this
For endless spiritual endowment
Beside it is a chalice
Drink from this
For this is holy
Unlike the cup
That runneth over with iniquity
Which some drink from
And see fun
These are the lost ones
Led astray
Far gone away
From the order for the day.

PLAY THIS

Play this
Until it's playlisted
Play this
Until it's A-listed
Play this
Then tell them who played it
Then
Tell them who made it
Play this
Until the case is all cracked
And the inlay is faded
Just play it
Play it
Until you can say it
Off by heart
Play it all the way until the end
And then back to the start
Again
Play it to all your friends
And if you've got enemies
Then play it for them
Play it in the house
In the car
At work

Or on the road
Play it loud
So everybody knows
What I'm saying
And what's playing
Play it, yo
Because spoken word
Doesn't really get to rock the radio
So
We're going to have to let them know
To play it
And if anyone
Seems concerned
At how much its selling
Let them know
It's selling
And tell them
What you paid to take it
Was nothing compared
To what it costs to make it
And if they would dare to slate it
Then they're probably not very creative
Besides
Do you really think they could make this
Please
Play this

Play this for every artist
Everywhere across the globe
Who knows what it's like
To sleep at a bus station in the cold
In another city
Miles away from home
Just because they know
They had to be at the show
Just so they could sell some CDs
And make some dough
Just so they could eat
And pay rent
Or get kicked out onto the road
Let me hear you play this
Full time spoken word artists
Should be among the first to blast this
Those who work the hardest
Don't watch no face
Time will show where your heart is
And all shall be rewarded
According to their works
So play this
If you know
What the words are really worth
I don't really care
What you wear

Or what you do with you hair
I just want to caress your ear
So come closer
So I can touch you...there
Can you feel me?
Good
Because I want to play
So turn me on
And play with me
In your
CD player
Then say a prayer
That I won't go away
But stay
And just play
Always
At least once everyday
So you'll never need to hunt
Or stray
For these words I say
Just play...this
And hear me when I say this
If I could only make one wish
It would be that you play this
For ages
Like your favourite CD

For an eternity
Allowing the sound
To linger
In your subconscious mind
Eternally
Because it's more of an issue
That you play this
Rather than if you're burning me
So whatever you need to do
Just do
Because through you
They will learn of me
That's if
They haven't already heard of me
Either way
Just put in a good word for me
And tell them to play this
Tell them to play this
Like Nat Turner played slave masters
Play it to death
Tell them to play this
Like revolution
On a Rosa Parks bus
Because I ain't budging
Even if it means my last breath
Tell them to play this

Like Harriet Tubman
Played the underground
Leading the good people to my sound
It's most profound
Tell them all to gather around
And play this
In the fight for the needy peoples
Play this
Like Stevie and The Beatles
Play this
Like it's a number one hit
And you can't wait
For me to spit a sequel
Play this
Like you know it's hard to equal
Play this
Like I always
Come through with the treacle
Tell them
I hope it isn't too sweet for you
And tell those other poets
I said
I never came to compete with you
Because I would beat you
I rather meet with you
And build with you

Chill with you
But if you think
You're my lyrical murderer
I will have to kill you
Play this for them
And put it on repeat
So it plays again
Just to make sure
It plays for all those
Who don't invite me
To do their shows anymore
Think they're too nice now
So they try to close their doors
Don't think they realise
That I've been here before
And that when they're all gone
I'll still be here some more
Playing this for you
And if I said it
I say it because it's true
So play this
Play this
Like it's your favourite flavour
Taste this
Like the rest are tasteless
And this

You just want to savour
Lick your lips
And play this
For a player hater
Tell him the dish is delicious
And you are playing this
In honour of the caterer
The maker
The creator
And the recipe
Just keeps getting greater
For sure
Something they'll all adore
And the hungry crowd
Are saying
Please, sir
Can we have some more?
And it's me in the lab
With the G4
Cooking up concoctions
And formulas galore
Beats and lyrics
Pouring out all over the floor
Look what I made for you
What are you waiting for?
I find it quite outrageous

That I should even have to say this
When you already know
What you should do
And that you
Should just
Play
This.

RETURN TO SENDER

It remains evident to me
That some poets
Still can't understand my frequencies
Like they fail to comprehend
That the best thing
Is to leave me be
And stop trying to cause interference
If their visions were set in the right place
Then they would quite clearly see
Past their distorted minds
To a much clearer picture
And they would find
That I've got much better things
To do with my time
Than play silly down the alley
No time for dilly-dallying
Haven't been able to keep still
Since I took that trip down the valley
And ever since I got my act together
Poets find me challenging
But instead of trying to challenge him
You should be channelling
Tuning your channel in
For a better understanding

That I am not a game
That you and I
Are not the same
You just can't be like me
And that's a shame
But I am not to blame
It was meant for me to be this way
Since the day I came
And believe me
I will not change
It's strange
How you claim to know
Much better poets than me
But discreetly
You keep calling out my name
Yes
You have no secrets
Your confidants
Are like loudspeakers
So you should watch who you speak with
And keep with
Because some become foes
When things get a little heated
Prepared to throw stones
Then you should also
Be ready to be defeated

I can sense weakness
When you
Should've had your Weetabix
How dare you
Try to compete with this
Clearly you're naive
To the spirits and deities I meet with
Whenever I breathe this
But do perceive this
If the half hearted scripts you spit
Are the much better definitions of poetry
We don't want to buy it
You can keep it
We don't need it
We prefer our prose a little deeper
Our flows a lot sweeter
Poet, you're not hot
Someone's been misleading you
You need to stop
Eating whatever it is they're feeding you
It's rot
Stale like your fifteen minute poetry slots
We admire poets who rock mics
With insight
You just recite
And read a lot

You're not inspiring
Just tiring
Sending audiences to sleep a lot
Look
To be honest
I didn't even want to be here today
I was quite happy
Going along peacefully on my way
But a door was opened
And someone had something to say
And it wasn't in my favour
Another nobody poet
Seeking fame off of my flavour
And that part is okay
Artists
Have been doing that with me for years
The pleasure is more mine than theirs
But the problem is
When you do it
By putting me down in front of your peers
That's a no go
But you've already gone there
So
That's why we're here
Listen
I know poets

Who recite poems
That make people want to go home
And make serious changes in their life
I know poets
Who recite poems
That make people want to go home
And make sweet love
To their husband or their wife
I know poets
Who recite poems
With a pain to make tears
Well up in your eyes
I know poets
Who recite poems
That'll still have you laughing
The following night
I've heard poets recite poems
That have people travelling distances
To hear twice
Because they were so nice
And then there's you
Still boring audiences to death
And we don't care
Where on this globe
You go to perform, bro
We still aren't impressed

Anyone who thinks
You are saying something
Obviously hasn't heard us yet
Because if they did
Then they would know
That you just aren't worth the listening
And all the people I know
Who've heard you
Need more convincing
Well
He sounds ok
But he should really stick to the page
You get a little hype and a little name
And now you want to bring it to the stage
What, you're still mad
Because we went head to head
In a two minute slam
And I beat you
Bro, wasn't that years ago
Or is it because my CDs sell
And yours don't
I thought we were grown
In fact
You're older than me
But you act like a girl I said no to
Can't get what you want

So now look what you go and do
Look
What you make me have to go through
Just to show you
There's some things
You just don't say
And don't do
And by the way
Your little malicious email
Never moved me
More amused me
And may those gathered here today
Please excuse me
But this is what happens
When another poet is rude to me
And treats me unruly
Thinking he has the right
To interfere with my mic
Disrespecting the grind
Disregarding the fact
That this
Is how me and mine
Eat at night
Keep on the light
Heat up the pipe
And sleep at night

Angry
Because he put out the book
And the CDs
And launched the website
And still can't get the formula right
Somebody please
Give the brother a hug
He seems a little uptight
Frustrated
Trying to bring me down
So that he can take flight
Trying to dim my shine
So that we can notice his light
But if you notice
It's not too bright
Hard to notice
Much like
A firefly
On a bonfire
On fireworks night
What is he like
Now he's trying to disrespect me
In his poetry when he writes
But that's not nice
I remember when
You were putting on

Your first little shows
By yourself
I used to turn up to the venue
When you were setting up
And asked you if you wanted any help
When you had no-one else
And this is the thanks I get
Well I'm back again
To help you finish making your bed
I'm going to make sure you regret
Every single word that you said
Don't you forget
And please don't fret
For all shall be fair
Once I return to sender
We are birds of a different feather
And you're going to learn to remember
And those poets
That you think are feeling you
They're not
Come on
Let's be serious
They're only feeling
What they think you can do
For their careers
And crowd

Don't be fooled
Everything is not as it appears
We need to really watch
And listen
Really use our ears
Do some poets even really care
Do they even really want to know
It's only when they're performing
That you see them at the show
Doing their thing
Then they go
And they don't even come to our shows
But with myself you know
I don't even have to be performing
But I'll be there
Sitting right in the front row
Supporting
But some of these poets
No
It's all about ego
And so
He figured he'd go
Criticise me
Knowing he hasn't got what it takes
To get beside me
So he decides to get beside himself

Dropping remarks
Unwilling to acknowledge the heart
I put into my art
Instead he throws darts
Trying to create sparks
But someone should tell him
That's how a fire starts
And spreads
And I will not be the one
Bearing the scars
My friend
Please depart from my path
And let us not have to come back here
Again.

THE BATTLE

I hope you've got some
Super fancy
Fantastic tricks up your sleeve
If not
I think it's about your time to leave
Because I'm about to stampede
Over weak MC's
Like a herd of cattle
And my advice is think twice
If you're considering a battle
Because you
Just couldn't withstand the pressure
I bring it to you measure by measure
For you it would be pain
For me it's pleasure
I do this for leisure
And I can never resist
Breaking an MC down to the ground
Without raising a fist
For me it's pure bliss
For you it's dangerous
You had the chance to leave
But you had to persist
Now you face

The consequences of this
You made a big mistake
Thinking you could take me out
Now I'm about to show you
What taking out is all about
You should have closed your mouth
And listened
Now you can feel the power
Of my ammunition
As I off-load
And take your whole shit
Off the road
With one blow
Watch it explode
You should have known
And if you don't know
I'll make you know
It's Phenzwaan
Telling you so to your face
Against me
You're out of place
And a waste of space
Against me
You're a disgrace
Your attacks are useless
And futile

In fact to battle me
You need a new style
I'm too wild
And hard to handle
I come at you
From all angles
A lyrical vandal
I'll leave your whole shit
Dismantled.

THE DRAGNET

Poets want to test me
But who could ever step to me
Been too hot
Since god blew breath in me
And I will be until the death of me
I rock mics professionally
Bring me to wherever your session be
Especially
Since I've got the key to what you seek
Watch what you say to me
When you speak
Please
I've had this locked
Long before I dropped the first CDs
Don't get it twisted
This one is another hit
I never left
And even in death
I remain enlisted
A soldier
Cursed and gifted
What are your words worth
Against the verse
That crowds came out to witness

This is it
When I dismiss the swiftest
When I spit this
Lyrics spread across the globe
Like sickness
Act like you know
I'm not hard to find
You got beef with me
I'll be at home
Probably in the lab writing a rhyme
About my neighbourhood
And how it's no good
How easy it is
For kids to buy and sell crack now
Or how easy it is to get a Gat now
How my brothers
Seem to be dying in packs now
Or how life is still harder
If you're male or female
Young and black now
I'm from the Hack town
Where brothers don't back down
Drag you off stage
If you haven't got your rap down
So who's the next act now
You're not rappers

You're actors
And you're not a poet
You're a clown
With weak lyrics
And a whole heap of gimmicks
Watch how quick
Your careers diminish
I was here
Long before you came to town
I'm everywhere
And I'll still be here
When you're not around
Spectators love my sound
In places you can't even pronounce
Let me see you bounce
I want to hear you praising my name
You know why I came
We are not the same
Be careful what you say
I'm in this to win
I haven't got time for the games
I don't play
And if you aren't behind me
Or alongside me
Then get out of my way
Or get caught up in my dragnet

Set for all those who disrespect
I disconnect
Reconnect
And you still ain't saying nothing yet
But you owe me
So I've come to collect
Homie
And if you know me
Then you know I don't pet
So what you say
You might live to regret
Because I decipher the indirect
And check you
Do you even know who you're next to
Those people you're talking to
Don't even respect you
See how your secrets
Just spread to the next dude
And the next dude
Man, forget you
Your weak words won't protect you
When mine start to wet you
They say I'm the one
I bring thunder
And lightning when I come
I'm too tight when I write

You come undone
Like new shoe laces
I rock mics
In new and old school places
Because I got too much flavour
You're just tasteless
How dare you
Come up against this
I was made for this
So I slaved for this
When you'd forsaken this
Look where I've taken this
You ain't got no place in this
You're just faking this
Stay gone
Don't show your face in this
Or start what you can't finish
My heart is still in this
And it's still business
And I still win this
And so far
I haven't sparked one spliff
The heavenly flow
Is already high
And oh so nat-ur-el
But if you step out of line, bro

It will give you hell
And who could tell
I would do it this well
Haters are pissed to know my CDs sell
And I haven't even started yet
Seas haven't even been parted yet
Speaking of which
Some poets flows are wet
Better keep their selves in check
And critics can rate me as a poet
But I'm an architect
And my target
And my market's set
I'm one of the smartest yet
I'm one of the last that's left
So now poets want to start to test
With no heart in their chest
I spit darts
Until they gasp for breath
Because if I ever left
The scene would starve to death
And no I'm not done
Like I said
I haven't even started yet
Got lots more in store
For that G4

Beats and lyrics
Pouring out all over the floor.

THE SETTLEMENT

Here we go again
Another CD, see
The volume final
And indeed
We will survive
Regardless
Of all the stress and strife
This life provides
Don't ask me how
Ask me why
It's imperative we do
Or it's definite we die
It's a hard road for the wicked
Even harder for the wise
My goal is to make souls cry
In the hope that it opens eyes
To focus and rise
In this life
Anything is possible if you try
So never be afraid to shine
Me, I came a long way
In a short space of time
Because I work hard
Made myself fortunate

To bless the world with my rhymes
And so far
These words have spread
From London to Cairo
New York to Toronto
Germany
Japan
Barbados
Italy
Ghana
Australia
Phenzwaan won't be failing ya'
This is just the tip of the iceberg
And that's my word
I'm in this for the long haul
See, in this life
It's your call
You can create the court
And the ball
Do it with your whole heart
Or not at all
Nothing big is ever accomplished
By playing small
You start achieving
When you start believing
But there's no point pretending

If you aren't ready
To bring the proper action
To back it up
And if you're sitting down
Thinking its all going to fall in your lap
Then you need to get your act up
Like you know
You've got what it takes for this
And I won't embarrass people
And start mentioning names
But you really need to stop faking it
When you could be making it
You already created a place in it
So stop wasting it
With this procrastinating
Shit
We're building
Stronger foundations in this
While you're shaking it to bits
Ain't that a bitch
Half these half-hearted poets
Need to get their minds fixed
Running around
Talking behind other poets backs
And all that
We haven't got time for it

Too busy shining
Like it's our last day on the planet
And it's heavy work
Don't hate us because you can't manage
And I don't think you plan to fail
I just think you fail to plan it
Got nothing but love for you
But step up to these mics against us
And we'll just step right up after
And do you some damage
Funny how one poem
Can make a few poets vanish
And my language isn't Spanish
So understand this
Is Phenzology
You're in tune
To an appliance of science
Right here
That will open your mind
If you open your ears
Get you in gear for future years
On top of a life
Already filled with tears
Survival is relinquishing fears
Are you prepared
It's no joke out here

Get serious
Stop playing around
If you say you're truly representing
If you're truly doing this
For the betterment
Let's start seeing some evidence
Come join this young lyrical president
And let's build on this thing
We're already residents
For real
You know the deal
Don't speak if I don't feel it's relevant
So rewind this track right here
And signed
Sealed
Delivered
It's yours
The Settlement.

THE WORLD IS GETTING MAD

Hey yo'
Forget my dress code
Because my clothes
Aren't taking us home
From the storm
Let it be known
This day a shining star was born
Phenzwaan
And what I wear
Don't watch that
Because I will still perform my duty
And shine
Look
Our babies are dying
In the street
No time to scrutinise my feet
Want to watch something
Watch me ride the beat
Trying to up-rise
The minds of the weak
And poor
In this mental war
This is more than beginning
We've been here before

148

Opposition winning
Got mad points
We're here to even the score
Don't want to join forces
Then what are you here for
Not sure?
Then step to the back
Real soldiers
Step forward
Upfront for attack
We're about to take our shit back
Into our own rightful hands
What part of revolution
Don't you understand?
We ain't got shit
Because they got it
And trying to knock us with it
Get smart
Who's got the drugs money?
Who's got the guns money?
Who's got the plane and ship money?
Who the hell thinks this is funny?
We're struggling for cash
Little Jermaine
Just got shot down over crack
By another pusher

Nicknamed Green Eye
Who fired four times
Rat-ta-tat-tat-tat
Now he's about to face life for that
Where are brothers and sisters minds at?
Do we care?
Now Tina lays dead in the club
Over a pair of Nike Air.

YOU MIGHT DIE HERE

Now
Mastering how to succeed
In getting through it
May undoubtedly
Require a higher branch of knowledge
But in all your years here to be
I can definitely assure you
That you will never need
A GCSE
Degree
PHD
TV
PC
Or even an STD
To see
Just how hard this life is
For you or your kids
Because, you see
This entire world
Is teaching it for free
Just take a look out
Into the street
And see
I mean

The truth is
You just might die here
Right here
Right now
If not in flesh
Then in spirit
And somehow
Whenever death takes the soul
Many know
The physical body
Often follows with it
I'll tell you
The rougher this life is getting
Tougher still
Must be your will to live it
And if like me
You've ever taken a step back
To analyse the ills of this world
Then you've seen some sick shit
Shit that hurts
That has gone from bad to worse
That needs to get better
That needs to heal
Like carpet burns
Like parasitic worms
Like bad perms

Or worse still
Like the drug dealer
That hasn't learned
That being black
And selling drugs
Is the best way to see
That you or me
Never become
Or remain rich
In any sense of the word
It's like nobody told him
Or he hasn't heard
That these DRUGS
Are
Destroying
Righteousness
Unto
Gods
Servants
Like nobody told him
Or he just didn't listen
When somebody mentioned
That after the demise
Of drug dealing partnerships
With the police
That he would end up in prison

The cage
Where he's now currently living
Meanwhile
I'm on a 253 bus
London
Listening
To my frustrated bro
On his mobile
Taking in
Another twenty minute dose
Of his baby mother's
Mind full of silly games
Handing out stress on a phone line
Along with confirmations
That she'll never change
And I'm urging him
To cut this
Dead end conversation
To try and save him
From the radiation
Seeping into his brain
And everyday is a strain
But we're keeping in charge
Of situations
Striving to maintain
Because if we don't

Our souls might die here
And our children
Just the same.

ABOUT THE AUTHOR

Phoenix James is an award winning Writer, Poet, Author and Spoken Word Recording Artist. He began performing his poetic words live on stages across the UK in 1998. His debut spoken word poetry album, *The A.R.T.I.S.T*, was released in 2000. His first limited edition printed collection of poetry, *To Whom It May Concern,* was published in 2003. He has toured and performed his poetry internationally since 2004. He has appeared in films, on television and radio shows, and collaborated with other artists, singer-songwriters, actors, musicians, filmmakers and producers. In 2013, he wrote, directed and produced the feature length mock documentary film, *Love Freely but Pay for Sex*. Phoenix James has written, recorded and released several spoken word poetry albums including, *Phenzwaan Now & Forever* (2009), *A Patchwork Remedy for A Broken Melody* (2020), *FREE* (2021), *Haven for the Tormented* (2021), *With All That Said* (2022), and *Remixes* Volumes: 1 & 2 (2022).

If you enjoyed reading this book, please leave a review online. The author reads every review and they help new readers discover his work.

PHOENIX JAMES

Photo by Kersten Bower

Phoenix James lives in London, England.

Connect with Phoenix James on his online
social media platforms via www.linktr.ee/
Phoenix_James and say you've read this book.
To contact or learn more about Phoenix James
and his creative journey or to receive updates
via his Newsletter Mailing List, visit his official
website at www.PhoenixJamesOfficial.com

Phoenix James Official

www.ingramcontent.com/pod-product-compliance
Lightning Source LLC
Chambersburg PA
CBHW021233090426
42740CB00006B/515